Andrew
Brodie

Improving
Comprehension

for ages 6-7

A & C Black • London

Contents

Introduction

Improving Comprehension includes a range of interesting and exciting texts for sharing with pupils and using for reading comprehension. The texts have been carefully selected to be appropriate to the age group and to cover a range of text types. They reflect the demands of the Primary Framework for Literacy and in particular they following the learning objectives for Year 2. The accompanying comprehension worksheets are differentiated at three levels and are designed to be used by individuals or small groups. *Notes for teachers* are provided at the bottom of each worksheet providing guidance on how to get the most from the texts and how to approach the questions on the sheet.

For monitoring and recording purposes an *Individual record sheet* is provided on page 4 detailing reading and writing levels appropriate for Year 2. You may also find it helpful to refer to the *Contents* page where the 'texts' are linked to the relevant Assessment Focuses.

How to use the book and CD-ROM together

The book has fifteen 'texts', which can be projected on to a whiteboard for whole class use using the CD-ROM, or photocopied/printed for use with small groups or individuals. Sharing the text either on screen or on paper provides lots of opportunities for speaking and listening, for decoding words through a phonic approach, for reading and re-reading for meaning and for satisfaction and enjoyment in shared success.

For each text there are three comprehension worksheets at different ability levels to enable teachers to differentiate across the ability range. An animal picture at the top of the sheet indicates the level of the worksheet. The 'cat' exercises are at the simplest level; the 'dog' exercises are at the next level; the 'rabbit' exercises are at the most advanced level. You may decide to give some pupils the 'cat' worksheet and then decide, on the basis of their success, to ask them to complete the 'dog' worksheet. A similar approach could be taken with the 'dog' and 'rabbit' sheets.

After reading the text with the pupils the teacher should discuss the tasks with the children, ensuring that they understand clearly how to complete the worksheet and reminding them to answer the questions using full sentences and correct punctuation.

National Curriculum levels

The worksheets are aimed at the following ability levels:

Cat worksheets are for pupils working towards Level 1.
Dog worksheets are for pupils working at Level 1.
Rabbit worksheets are for pupils who are working confidently at Level 1 and are progressing towards Level 2.

Individual record sheet

Pupil's name: _____

Date of birth: _____

Reading Level 1

- [ ] I can recognise familiar words in simple texts.
- [ ] I can use my knowledge of letters and sound-symbol relationships in order to read words, sometimes with support.
- [ ] I can use my knowledge of letters and sound-symbol relationships to establish meaning when reading aloud, sometimes with support.
- [ ] I can express my response to poems, stories and non-fiction by identifying aspects I like.

Reading Level 2

- [ ] I can show understanding when reading simple texts.
- [ ] My reading of simple texts is generally accurate.
- [ ] I can express opinions about major events or ideas in stories, poems and non-fiction.
- [ ] I can use phonic skills in reading unfamiliar words and establishing meaning.
- [ ] I can use graphic skills in reading unfamiliar words and establishing meaning.
- [ ] I can use syntactic skills in reading unfamiliar words and establishing meaning.
- [ ] I can use contextual skills in reading unfamiliar words and establishing meaning.

Writing Level 1

- [ ] My writing communicates meaning through simple words and phrases.
- [ ] I am beginning to show awareness, in my reading or my writing, of how full stops are used.
- [ ] My letters are clearly shaped.
- [ ] My letters are correctly orientated.

Writing Level 2

- [ ] My narrative writing communicates meaning.
- [ ] My non-narrative writing communicates meaning.
- [ ] I use appropriate and interesting vocabulary.
- [ ] I show some awareness of the reader.
- [ ] I can write a sequence of sentences to show ideas developing.
- [ ] My sentences are sometimes demarcated by capital letters and full stops.
- [ ] Usually, I can spell simple, monosyllabic words correctly or spell a phonetically plausible alternative.
- [ ] My letters are accurately formed.
- [ ] My letters are consistent in size.

A visit to the zoo

Farid's class was going on a trip to the zoo.
He had a list of things to take:

packed
lunch

drink

coat

Farid checked to see if he had everything
on the list before he left home.

At school Farid lined up with his class and soon a big coach
arrived. Mrs Davis, the teacher, said they could get on. Farid
sat with his friend Jo. Farid and Jo talked all the way to the
zoo about what they wanted to see when they got there.

"I want to see the seals being fed,"
said Farid. "I've seen them before
and they're funny."

"I really want to see the gorillas,"
said Jo.

"Can we go there first?"

"We'll have to stay with our group and go where our teacher
tells us," said Farid.

The two boys talked about all the animals they hoped to see
until the coach stopped at the zoo. Farid and Jo were in
Mr Jupp's group.

"We must check the seals' feeding time to make sure that we
don't miss it," said Mr Jupp. "And then we will go and see
the gorillas."

Name: _____

Date: _____

Answer the questions by completing the sentences.

Who was going to the zoo?

_____ was going to the zoo.

What did all the children need to take with them?

The children needed to take a _____,

a _____ and a _____

How did the children travel to the zoo?

The children travelled to the zoo

_____

Answer these questions using full sentences.

What did Farid want to see?

_____

_____

What did Jo want to see?

_____

_____

What animals would you like to see if you visited a zoo?

_____

_____

Notes for teachers
Read the passage with the children helping them to understand what has happened in the story and why both Farid and Jo might be pleased with the outcome. Read the instructions and the questions with the children ensuring that they understand them, particularly as the questions are in the past tense. Discuss the final question with the children and where in the zoo their chosen animal might be found. As with all the questions, help them to compose their sentences orally before they write anything down.

Improving Comprehension 6-7 © A & C Black Publications Ltd. 2008

A visit to the zoo

Name: _____

Date: _____

What was the name of Farid's teacher?

_____

_____

Who was in charge of Farid's group?

_____

_____

Who did Farid sit with on the coach?

_____

_____

Which animals did the two boys want to see?

_____

_____

Which other animals do you think they might see at the zoo?

_____

_____

Write about your favourite animal.

_____

_____

_____

_____

Notes for teachers
Read the passage through with the children helping them to understand why Farid and Jo might be pleased
with the outcome. Help them to use appropriate handwriting and correct punctuation when writing sentences
for their answers. Discuss the final question with the children and see if they can give a reason for their choice.
They might need help in composing their sentences orally before they write anything down.

A visit to the zoo

Name: _____

Date: _____

What are the names of the two adults in the story?

_____

_____

What are the names of the two children in the story?

_____

_____

What did the two boys talk about on the
way to the zoo?

_____

_____

Why did Farid want to see the seals?

_____

_____

Why do you think both boys would be pleased when
Mr Jupp told them what they were going to do?

_____

_____

_____

On a separate piece of paper, write about the animals you
would like to see at the zoo. Can you explain why?

Notes for teachers
Read the passage through with the children and make sure they understand why the ending is a good one. If the children are fairly confident readers they could take turns to read out parts of the story. The children might need some help with the last two questions. Discuss the final question with them and compose some sentences orally before writing anything down.

A birthday present

Dad asked <u>Jon</u> what he would like for his birthday. Jon said he would really like a <u>bike</u> but his dad explained that a bike would cost too much money.

"That's all right," said Jon. "Can I have a football instead?"

Dad said that he could. Jon tried to look pleased but really he wanted a bike because his best friend <u>Danny</u> had a great <u>bike</u>.

On his birthday Jon had lots of cards and a few presents. The card from Danny had a picture of a boy riding a bike. Jon wished he had a bike.

Dad gave Jon his present. Jon knew what it was because it was round. He tore off the paper.

"Thanks Dad, that's great," he said.

"Shall we go outside and play with it?" said Dad.

Jon and his dad put their shoes on and went out into the back garden. Jon kicked the ball down the garden. It was a great ball. It went behind the shed. Jon went to get the ball back. He saw something leaning on the back of the shed. It was a

big box.

"What's that?" said Jon.

"Open it and see," said Dad.

Jon tugged at the box. At last he opened it. Inside was ...

... the best bike in the world!

A birthday present

Name: _____

Date: _____

What did Jon want for his birthday?

Jon wanted _____ for his birthday.

What did Dad say he would get for Jon?

Dad said he would get Jon a

_____

What was the name of Jon's best friend?

Jon's best friend was called _____

What did Jon get for his birthday?

_____

_____

What did Jon find behind the shed?

_____

_____

Draw something you would like for your birthday. Write about it.

_____

_____

_____

_____

Notes for teachers
Read the story with the children, drawing their attention to the speech marks and making sure they understand why they are used. In answering the fourth question, children would be correct if they said 'football' or 'bike' or both of these. Discuss the final question with the children and why they would like their chosen present. Help them to write down their ideas using correct punctuation.

A birthday present

Name: _____

Date: _____

Answer the questions by filling in the spaces.

Why did Jon's Dad say that Jon could not have a bike?

Jon's Dad explained that a bike _____

Why did Jon really want a bike?

Jon really wanted a bike because _____

_____

Write sentences to answer these questions.

Where did Jon's ball go when he kicked it?

_____

_____

What was in the big box that Jon found?

_____

_____

Can you remember the best present you have ever had?
Write about the present.

_____

_____

_____

_____

Notes for teachers
Read the passage through with the children and check that they have understood the story. Discuss the final question with the children and encourage them to compose some ideas orally before they write anything down. You could tell the children about the best present you ever had and what made it the best.

A birthday present

Name: _____

Date: _____

Answer the questions by using complete sentences.

Why did Jon say he would have a football instead of a bike?

_____

_____

How did Jon know what his dad's present was?

_____

_____

What did Jon and his dad do before they went into the garden?

_____

_____

Why did Jon and his dad go into the garden?

_____

_____

Think about how Jon must have felt when he found the bike. Try to describe his feelings.

_____

_____

_____

Notes for teachers
Read the story with the children and make sure they understand the sequence of events. Ask the children to find which of the instructions above is not actually a question. How can they tell that it's not a question. The children might need some help in structuring an answer to the first question so discuss it before they write anything down. Similarly, with the final question, give the children a chance to articulate their ideas before writing their response and then help them to use neat handwriting and correct punctuation.

Improving Comprehension 6-7 © A & C Black Publications Ltd. 2008

Going on a train

"Platform 5 for the nine fifteen train to London
Paddington," said a loud voice. Kate
was very happy. She was standing on
Taunton Station waiting for the train to
London.

"Here it comes," said Mum.

Kate could see the train coming. It was
blue, white and pink. It was very long. They waited for the
train to stop. When it stopped, a door near Kate and Mum
opened and a man got out. Kate and her mum got in.

"Our tickets are for seats 9F and 9B," said Mum.

They looked for seats 9F and 9B. They found them but two
men were sitting in them.

"Excuse me," said Mum. "I think these are our seats."

The men looked at their tickets.

"Oh, sorry!" said one man.

"You are right," said the other man. "We should be in seats
8F and 8B."

The men moved so Kate and her mum could sit down.

"Why are the seats 9F and 9B?" asked Kate. "Why aren't
they 9A and 9B?"

"The F is for facing the front and the B
is for facing the back," explained Mum.

"I'm lucky. I'm facing the front," said
Kate.

Kate couldn't wait for the train to start
and for the journey to begin.

Improving Comprehension 6-7 © A & C Black Publications Ltd. 2008

Going on a train

Name: _____

Date: _____

Answer the questions by completing the sentences.

Where was Kate at the beginning of the story?

Kate was at the railway_____

What was Kate waiting for?

Kate was waiting for _____

_____

What colour was the train?

The train was _____, _____and _____

Write sentences to answer these questions.

Which seats did Kate and her Mum have?

_____

_____

Why was Kate lucky?

_____

_____

Have you ever been on a train? Where did you go?

_____

_____

_____

Notes for teachers
Read the story with the children and ask them to explain in their own words what happened. Encourage the children to answer the second question with more than just the word 'train' i.e. 'Kate was waiting for the train to London.' Discuss the last question with the children before they write anything down, encouraging them to write interesting and well-structured sentences.

Improving Comprehension 6-7 © A & C Black Publications Ltd. 2008

Name: _____

Date: _____

Answer the questions by completing the sentences.

Where was Kate at the beginning of the story?

Kate was _____

Where was the train going to?

The train _____

What was the train like?

The train was _____

Write sentences to answer these questions.

When they got on the train why didn't Kate and her mum sit down straight away?

_____

_____

What does the letter F on the ticket mean?

_____

_____

On a separate piece of paper, write about a journey you have had on a train or a bus.

Going on a train

Name: _____

Date: _____

Write sentences to answer these questions.

How did Kate feel at the start of the story? Explain why she felt like this.

_____

_____

_____

At what time was the train due at Taunton Station?

_____

_____

Which station was the train going to?

_____

_____

How did the men know they were in the wrong seats?

_____

_____

_____

On a separate piece of paper describe the last time you went on public transport.

Notes for teachers
Point out to the children that some of the questions could have more than one correct answer e.g. the men knew they were in the wrong seats because Kate's mum told them and because they had different numbers on their tickets. Explain that 'public transport' is any form of transport that follows a particular route and has set fares, e.g. trains, buses, trams, ferries, etc. If some children haven't been on public transport they could write about a car journey instead.

Improving Comprehension 6-7 © A & C Black Publications Ltd. 2008

On the train

Kate and her mum were on the train to London. This was Kate's first ride on a train. She was very excited.

"Tickets please," called a man. Mum got the tickets out of her bag. The man checked the tickets. He made small round holes in them with a hole-punch.

Kate looked out of the window. They were going very fast. The train was travelling on a high bank so Kate could look down at the fields.

"What can you see?" asked Mum.

"I can see the shadow of the train on the ground," said Kate.

"Oh yes!" said Mum. "You are good at spotting things. What else can you see?"

"Lots of things," said Kate. "I can see houses, trees, fields, fences, birds. I can see cows in a field."

"Look, there's a deer!" said Mum.

Kate missed it. The train was going very fast.

"There's a river with boats on," said Kate.

"That's not a river, it's a canal," said Mum.

Kate saw a boy on a boat. He was waving to the train. Kate waved back.

"Not long to go now," said Mum.

Improving Comprehension 6-7 © A & C Black Publications Ltd. 2008

On the train

Answer the questions by completing the sentences.

Were Kate and her mum on a bus, a train or a ferry?

Kate and her mum were on _____

How did Kate feel?

Kate was feeling _____

Where did Mum keep the tickets?

Mum kept the tickets

_____

Write sentences to answer these questions.

What could Kate see?

_____

_____

What did Mum see?

_____

_____

Look out of the window. What can you see?

_____

_____

_____

Notes for teachers
Help the children to read the passage using their phonic skills to decode any unfamiliar words. The children
might need help with the final question. Encourage them to observe carefully by asking questions such as
'What can you see on the ground?' 'What can you see in the sky?'

Improving Comprehension 6-7 © A & C Black Publications Ltd. 2008

On the train

Name: _____

Date: _____

Answer the questions by completing the sentences.

What were Kate and her mum doing?

Kate and her mum_____

_____

What did the man ask for?

The man _____

Write sentences to answer these questions.

Kate saw lots of things. Write down three of the things that Kate saw.

_____

_____

Kate thought she saw a river but what was it really?

_____

_____

Where was the boy?

_____

_____

On a separate piece of paper write about what you saw the last time you went on a journey.

Notes for teachers
Help the children to answer the third question by giving them the sentence starter 'On her train journey Kate saw......' Discuss the final task with the children encouraging them to think carefully about their last journey – it could have been on a train, bus, boat, aeroplane or in a car. As with all the questions, help them to compose their sentences orally before they write them down.

On the train

Name: _____

Date: _____

Write sentences to answer these questions.

What did the man do to the tickets? Can you explain why?

_____

_____

_____

How could Kate look down at the fields?

_____

_____

What do you think the weather was like?

_____

_____

Why did Kate miss seeing the deer?

_____

_____

Describe a journey you have made.

_____

_____

_____

_____

Notes for teachers
Read the questions with the children ensuring that they understand them, particularly the third and fourth questions where they will need to use inference to answer them. Discuss the final question with the children encouraging them to think carefully about a journey – it could have been on a train, bus, boat, aeroplane or in a car. As with all the questions, help them to compose their sentences orally before they write them down.

The wobbly tooth

Mel had a wobbly tooth. It was her very first wobbly tooth and she was very excited about it. On the first day it just felt a little loose and wobbly.

"I wish it would fall out," said Mel. She told her mum and dad about it. On the second day it wobbled a bit more.

"I wish it would fall out," said Mel. She told her teacher about it. She liked the feeling of it moving about in her mouth. She wobbled it with her tongue.

On the third day Mel told her friends about it.

"I wish it would fall out," said Mel.

She wiggled it with her finger. On the fourth day it was very loose indeed. She told her granny about it.

Mel began to worry a bit about it falling out. What if it hurt when it came out? What if she ate it by mistake? What if it came out when she was in the swimming pool or at a friend's house? Suddenly Mel wished her tooth wasn't wobbly anymore.

She told Granny about her worries. Granny smiled. She gave Mel a juicy apple to eat. Mel liked apples. She took a big bite of the apple. As she bit the apple the wobbly tooth came out. She looked at the tooth and smiled at Granny. Granny got a mirror so that Mel could see the space where the tooth had been. Mel hoped another tooth would be wobbly soon.

Improving Comprehension 6-7 © A & C Black Publications Ltd. 2008

The wobbly tooth

Name: _____

Date: _____

Put a ring round each of the correct answers.

Who had a wobbly tooth?

Mal   Mel   Mina   Mum

What did Granny give Mel to eat?

chocolate   a biscuit   a tooth   an apple

Who did she tell on the first day?

Her teacher   Her mum   Her friends   Her granny
and dad

Fill in the spaces in these sentences.

Mel wobbled the loose tooth with her_____.

She _____ it with her finger.

On a separate piece of paper draw a
picture of Mel looking in a mirror after
her tooth had come out. Write about
the picture.

Notes for teachers
Read the passage with the children helping them to use their phonic skills to decode unfamiliar words. The final question is to promote discussion and could be used as a speaking and listening activity. You could talk about what it feels like to have a wobbly tooth and how it feels once the tooth has come out. 'How does Mel look without her tooth?' 'What do you thing she will do with it?' Encourage children to write one or two clear sentences using capital letters and full stops in the correct places.

Improving Comprehension 6-7 © A & C Black Publications Ltd. 2008

Name: _____

Date: _____

Complete the sentences by filling in the gaps.

Mel was very _____ when she had a wobbly

_____. She wished that it would

_____. The tooth came out when

she _____.

Answer the next questions by writing a whole sentence for each one.

Who gave Mel an apple to eat?

_____

_____

How did Mel feel about her wobbly tooth on the first day?

_____

_____

How did Mel feel about her wobbly tooth on the fourth day?

_____

_____

On a separate piece of paper write about what you will do when you have a wobbly tooth. Draw a picture to go with your answer.

Notes for teachers
Talk about the final question with the children before they write anything down. Most children have lots of stories to tell about wobbly teeth! When they are ready, help them to write down their ideas using correct punctuation and spelling.

Improving Comprehension 6-7 © A & C Black Publications Ltd. 2008

The wobbly tooth

Name: _____

Date: _____

Name three things Mel worried about.

1 _____

2 _____

3 _____

How did Mel feel at the end of the story?

_____

_____

Why do think she felt like this?

_____

_____

Complete each of the following sentences in your own words to tell the story of the wobbly tooth.

When Mel found she had a wobbly tooth she

_____

_____

On the second day she _____

On the third day she _____

On the fourth day _____

Granny helped by _____

Improving Comprehension 6-7 © A & C Black Publications Ltd. 2008

Going to the dentist

I like to see the dentist.
He smiles then checks my teeth.
He makes sure they are shiny,
With no aches or pains beneath.

I climb onto his leather chair
He makes it rise so high.
I see the brightly shining lights
That made me shut my eyes.

When I lay back upon the chair
In front I see my toes.
And when looking at the dentist
I can see right up his nose.

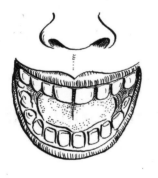

I like looking at the ceiling,
As I lay back on the chair.
A picture and some mobiles,
He has cleverly fixed up there.

The dentist says, "Just open wide,
So that I can look today
At your shiny, well looked after teeth
Then you can go away."

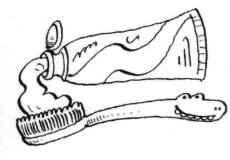

Then off I go, because I know
That brushing day and night,
Will keep my most amazing teeth
Clean, shiny, strong and white.

Going to the dentist

Name: _____

Date: _____

Put a ring round each of the correct answers.

The poem is about a visit to the

doctor   supermarket   cinema   dentist

The chair is made of

leather   paper   cloth   plastic

What is fixed to the ceiling?

lights and bells   picture and mobiles   toes and nose

Complete these sentences by filling in the gaps.

The dentist makes sure that the teeth are _____, with no aches or pains.

The person in the poem brushes her teeth each morning and each _____

Draw a picture of you cleaning your teeth. Write about your picture.

_____

_____

_____

_____

Notes for teachers
Read the poem with the children and talk about how it works as rhyming verse. Discuss their ideas for the final question before they write anything down. Encourage the children to write one or two clear sentences using capital letters and full stops in the correct places.

Going to the dentist

Name: _____

Date: _____

Complete these sentences by filling in the gaps.

The dentist tells the child that after having her teeth looked

at she will be able to_____ .

There is a _____ and some

_____ fixed to the _____ .

Answer the next questions by writing a whole sentence for each one.

Why is the girl visiting the dentist?

_____

_____

How often does the girl in the poem brush her teeth?

_____

_____

Is the dentist cheerful or sad? Explain how you know this.

_____

_____

Look in the poem to find the words that rhyme with each of words below.

today   _____   there   _____

toes   _____   night   _____

Notes for teachers
Read the poem with the children and talk about the rhyming words. They might notice that 'high' and 'eyes' is only a half rhyme. The final task can provide an opportunity to look more generally at rhyming words and how the sound is the important aspect of the rhyming whilst the spelling pattern at the end of the word might well be different. As an extension activity ask the children whether they liked the poem or not. Can they give reasons for their answer?

Going to the dentist

Name: _____

Date: _____

Which four words are used in the last verse to describe the girl's teeth? The answer has been started for you.

The four words used to describe _____

_____

_____

Name three ways that you know the text is a poem.

1 _____

2 _____

3 _____

Join the first part of each sentence to the correct second part. The first one has been done for you.

I need to go to the		see up his nose.
When I am in the chair I can		twice a day so they are kept beautifully clean.
The dentist asks me to		dentist to have my teeth checked.
I brush my teeth		open my mouth so he can look at my teeth.

On a separate piece of paper draw and label a picture of a dentist checking your teeth.

Notes for teachers
The first question enables you to do some simple work on adjectives if time allows. The three things that children should notice that identify the text as a poem are: The rhyming words at the ends of the 2nd and 4th line of each verse; the capital letter at the beginning of each line; and the layout of the text in verses.
The final question allows work to be done on labelling and encourages discussion on what pupils know about dental surgeries.

Ring, ring

Ring, ring.

"Hello," said Mum.

"Who is it?" said Dad.

"Sh!" said Mum.

"Who is it?" said Stella.

"Sh!" said Mum.

"Who is it?" said Ben.

"Sh!" said Mum.

"That will be lovely," said

Mum. "Goodbye," she said.

"Who was it?" said Dad.

"Gran," said Mum.

"What did she say?" said Ben.

"She's coming to stay," said Mum.

"Hooray!" said Stella and Ben.

Improving Comprehension 6-7 © A & C Black Publications Ltd. 2008

Ring, ring

Answer the questions by filling in the spaces.

Who answered the telephone?

_____answered the telephone.

What did Mum say first?

Mum said _____.

Who was Mum talking to on the phone?

Mum was talking to

_____.

What was the name of the girl?

The girl was called _____.

What was the name of the boy?

The boy was called _____.

Write a sentence to answer this question.

Why did Gran ring to speak to Mum?

_____

_____

_____

Notes for adults
Read the passage through to the children helping them to understand what has happened in the conversation and that it is a conversation. Point out the use of speech marks to show the words that are spoken. With the second question show them how to use the speech marks to indicate what Mum said. The final question is particularly difficult and the children may need lots of help, both in working out the answer and in expressing it in a clear sentence.

Improving Comprehension 6-7 © A & C Black Publications Ltd. 2008

Ring, ring	Name: _____
	Date: _____

Complete the sentences to answer the questions.

Who answered the telephone when it rang?

Mum _____

_____

What did Dad say?

Dad said _____

What were the names of the two children?

The two children _____

_____

Write complete sentences to answer these questions.

Who was on the phone to Mum?

_____

What does Gran plan to do?

_____

_____

How did the children feel about the news?

_____

_____

Notes for teachers
Read the passage through to the children helping them to understand what has happened in the conversation. Point out the use of speech marks to show the words that were spoken. Help the children with the questions, ensuring that they use complete sentences to answer them e.g. we have effectively provided the answer to the first question but the child's task here is to complete the sentence with appropriate punctuation.

Improving Comprehension 6-7 © A & C Black Publications Ltd. 2008

Ring, ring

Name: _____

Date: _____

Write sentences to answer these questions.

Why did Mum keep saying 'Sh!'?

_____

_____

The caller is a member of the family.
What relation is she to the children?

_____

_____

What relation do you think she is to Mum?

_____

_____

What news has Gran given to Mum?

_____

_____

Who is pleased about the news?

_____

_____

Write about your family.

_____

_____

Notes for teachers
Read the passage through to the children helping them to understand what has happened in the conversation. Point out the use of speech marks to show the words that were spoken. Children might find the final task quite difficult as it is open ended, so first discuss family members with them before they write anything down.

Improving Comprehension 6-7 © A & C Black Publications Ltd. 2008

Jumping in

Jago stood on the side of the pool. He didn't want to jump in. He didn't like swimming.

"Jump in!" called the teacher.

The other children jumped in. Jago did not jump in. He did not want to jump in.

"Jump in Jago," said his teacher.

Jago looked at the tiles at the bottom. If he jumped in his feet might slip. He might bang his head on the side. He didn't want to jump in.

"Jump in Jago," said his teacher.

Jago looked at the water. If he jumped in his head might go under the water. He didn't want to jump in.

"Jump in Jago," said his teacher.

"Jump in Jago," said Yusuf.

"Jump in Jago," said Ella.

Jago bent his knees. He didn't want to jump in but he had to.

"I'll count to three," said his teacher. "One, … two, … three …"

Jago jumped in. There was a big splash. His feet felt the tiles at the bottom but he didn't slip. He didn't bang his head on the side. His head went under the water but it came back up again.

"Good boy!" said his teacher.

"Well done!" said Yusuf.

"Wow!" said Ella.

Jago smiled. He liked jumping in.

"Can I jump in again?" he said.

Improving Comprehension 6-7 © A & C Black Publications Ltd. 2008

Jumping in

Name: _____

Date: _____

Answer the questions by completing the sentences.

Where was Jago?

Jago was at the _____

_____

What did the teacher want Jago to do?

The teacher wanted Jago to _____

_____.

What are the names of Jago's friends?

Jago's friends are called _____

_____.

Write sentences to answer these questions.

Why didn't Jago want to jump in?

_____

_____

What did Yusuf say when Jago jumped in?

_____

_____

Do you like jumping in?

_____

_____

Improving Comprehension 6-7 © A & C Black Publications Ltd. 2008

Jumping in

Name: _____

Date: _____

Write sentences to answer the questions.

Where was Jago?

_____

_____

What did Jago think might happen if he
jumped in?

_____

_____

_____

Who was telling Jago to jump in?

_____

_____

What happened when Jago jumped in?

_____

_____

_____

At the end of the story how did Jago feel about jumping in?

_____

_____

_____

Notes for teachers
Read the passage with the children and see if they can explain what Jago was frightened of and how he overcame
his fear. Discuss the final question with the children and encourage them to write about Jago's feeling and why he
felt like that. Help them to write a well-structured sentence using the correct punctuation.

Improving Comprehension 6-7 © A & C Black Publications Ltd. 2008

Name: _____

Date: _____

Write sentences to answer the questions.

What did the teacher want Jago to do?

_____

_____

What did Jago think when he looked at the tiles at the bottom of the pool?

_____

_____

_____

How did the teacher encourage Jago to jump in?

_____

_____

What happened when Jago jumped in?

_____

_____

_____

What happened when you last went swimming?

_____

_____

_____

Notes for teachers
Read the passage through with the children helping them to understand what has happened in the story. Discuss the last question with the children. There may not have been any special incident but they could describe who they went with, what they practised, whether they enjoyed it, etc. Be prepared to think of another question if some children don't go swimming.

Improving Comprehension 6-7 © A & C Black Publications Ltd. 2008

Booster (Part 1)

Booster was a puppy, a big bouncy puppy.

Booster liked to run and he liked to bark.

He lived in a very small house.

He was starting to be a problem.

He knocked things over, he woke the baby and he frightened the postman.

Booster was tied up in the back yard where he couldn't get into trouble.

He was sad and lonely, and he barked and barked. No one liked the barking.

"It's no good," said Dad, "that dog must go!"

A van came to get Booster. He went away feeling frightened. He didn't know where he was going. Booster arrived in a new place.

Would this be his new home?

There were lots of other dogs there.

Some very kind people looked after them all.

Dogs came and dogs went.

Booster wondered where the dogs were going. He barked and barked.

Improving Comprehension 6-7 © A & C Black Publications Ltd. 2008

Name: _____

Date: _____

Put a ring round each of the correct answers.

What is the puppy's name?

Hooch   Scooby   Booster   Sophie

What sort of house did he live in?

large   small   tiny   tall

Who did the puppy frighten?

The postman   The baby   The puppy   The children

Answer the next questions by filling in the spaces.

Booster liked to _____ and to _____.

He was taken away in a _____.

Draw a picture of you with a dog that you would like.
Write about your picture.

_____

_____

_____

_____

_____

Notes for teachers

Read the passage with the children helping them to decode any unfamiliar words. The final question is to promote discussion and could be used as a speaking and listening exercise before the children write anything down. Encourage them to write one or two clear sentences using capital letters and full stops in the correct places.

Improving Comprehension 6-7 © A & C Black Publications Ltd. 2008

Booster (Part 1)

Name: _____

Date: _____

Answer the questions by completing the sentences.

Name two of the problems Booster caused.

Booster _____ the baby and _____

things over.

What is a puppy?

A puppy is a young _____.

Answer the next questions by writing whole sentences.

What did Booster do that no one liked?

_____

_____

Where did Booster see lots of other dogs?

_____

_____

Booster saw other dogs leaving the rescue centre. He
wondered where they were going. Where do you think they
were going?

_____

_____

Notes for teachers
Read the passage through with the children helping them to understand what has happened in the story. If you
feel that they are able to do so, help them to read it themselves by decoding the words using their phonic skills.
They might need some help answering the last question e.g. The other dogs were going to a new home with
kind owners. If appropriate, you could dictate this sentence for children to write down so they can practise
segmenting words for spelling.

Improving Comprehension 6-7 © A & C Black Publications Ltd. 2008

Booster (Part 1)

Name: _____

Date: _____

Why did Booster have to be tied up in the yard?

_____

_____

How did Booster feel when he was tied up in the yard?

_____

_____

What did he do in the yard?

_____

_____

When Booster was taken away, where was he taken?
Explain how you know this.

_____

_____

_____

This is only the first part of the story.

What might happen next?

Write an ending to the story on a separate piece of paper.

Notes for teachers
Ensure pupils don't have access to the final part of the text until they have completed the work on this page.
Explain to them that this is not a task that they can get right or wrong, they can just enjoy inventing their own
ending to the story.

Booster (Part 2)

One day a family came to meet Booster.
They made a fuss of him. Booster wagged his
tail. He barked a lot and bounced about. The
family patted him, stroked him and laughed
at him. Booster wished they were his family.

The family got ready to leave. Mr Mays put a new shiny collar
and lead on Booster.

Booster went with them to the car. The children got into the
back of the car. Mrs Mays got into the
front of the car. Mr Mays opened the back
seats of the car and Booster jumped in.
After a long ride the
car stopped and the

family got out. Mr Mays opened the back
of the car and Booster jumped out.
The family took Booster into the house.
He barked and ran from room to room.
He went out of the back door and raced
around the big garden outside. He barked and barked
and the family all laughed.

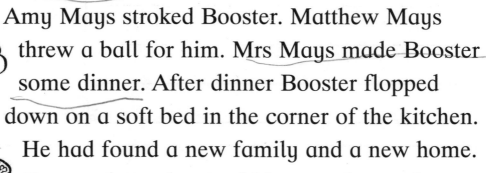

Amy Mays stroked Booster. Matthew Mays
threw a ball for him. Mrs Mays made Booster
some dinner. After dinner Booster flopped
down on a soft bed in the corner of the kitchen.
He had found a new family and a new home.
Booster knew he would be very happy here.

Name: _____

Date: _____

Put a ring round each of the correct answers.

What was the last name of the family who gave Booster a new home?

Mays   Mills   Moore   Morris

What was his new garden like?

small   tiny   green   big

What was new and shiny?

A car   A collar   A house   A bowl

Complete the sentences by filling in the gaps.

Booster _____ around his new garden.

Matthew threw a _____ for Booster.

Draw a picture of Booster playing with the children in his new home. Write about the picture.

_____

_____

_____

_____

Notes for teachers
Read the passage with the children helping them to understand what has happened to Booster in this second part of the story. The children might need some help with the writing task in the last question. Encourage them to write one or two clear sentences using capital letters and full stops in the correct places.

Improving Comprehension 6-7 © A & C Black Publications Ltd. 2008

Name: _____

Date: _____

Answer the questions by completing the sentences.

What did Booster wish when he met the Mays family?

Booster wished that _____

What did Mr Mays put on Booster?

Mr Mays put _____

_____

What were the names of the Mays children?

The children were called _____

Answer the next questions by writing whole sentences.

What did Booster do after tea?

_____

_____

What did Mrs Mays do for Booster?

_____

_____

What did the family do when Booster barked and barked?

_____

_____

Notes for teachers
Read the passage with the children helping them to understand what has happened to Booster in this second part of the story. If you feel that they are able to do so, help them to read it themselves by using their phonic skills to decode the words.

Name: _____

Date: _____

How did Booster feel when he first met the Mays family? Explain how you know this.

_____

_____

_____

How did Booster get out into the new garden?

_____

_____

How did Booster get from the rescue centre to his new home?

_____

_____

Why do you think Booster ran from room to room when he first went into the new house?

_____

_____

Write six words that you think describe Booster's character.

1 _____   4 _____

2 _____   5 _____

3 _____   6 _____

Improving Comprehension 6-7 © A & C Black Publications Ltd. 2008

Sheba and the dragon

There was once a sheep called Sheba. Sheba and all her friends liked to eat grass. They would eat grass all day long.

One day Sheba and her friends were eating grass in a big field. Sheba was chewing and chewing, munching and munching. She didn't see her friends go out of the field into the next field and then into another field. When Sheba stopped chewing she looked up. Her friends were gone!

Sheba looked round. Her friends were gone but in the field with Sheba was a big green dragon. "I like to eat sheep," said the big green dragon.

"I like to eat grass," said Sheba.

"I am very hungry," said the big green dragon.

"If you help me find my friends there will be lots of sheep," said Sheba. The dragon smiled a big dragon smile.

"Climb on my back," he said. Sheba climbed on the dragon's back and the dragon flew up into the sky. Sheba could see her friends now. "There they are!" she shouted.

The dragon flew down to the field. Sheba jumped off his back. The dragon licked his lips.

"I like to eat sheep," said the big green dragon.

"We like to eat grass," said the sheep. "Please don't eat us. Share our grass instead."

So the dragon tried the grass.

"That's good," said the big green dragon.

"Have some more," said the sheep.

So the dragon had some more.

"That's very good," said the big green dragon.

And from that day on the dragon lived with the sheep, eating grass just like they did.

Improving Comprehension 6-7 © A & C Black Publications Ltd. 2008

Sheba and the dragon

Name: _____

Date: _____

Answer the questions by finishing the sentences.

What was the name of the sheep?

The name of the sheep was _____

What colour was the dragon?

The dragon was _____

What did the sheep like to eat?

The sheep liked _____

_____

What did the dragon like to eat at the start of the story?

The dragon _____

_____

What did the dragon like to eat at the end of the story?

The dragon _____

_____

What do you like to eat?

_____

_____

Notes for teachers
Read the passage through with the children helping them to understand what has happened in the story and how the sheep ended up fooling the dragon. If you feel that they are able to do so, help them to read it themselves by decoding the words using their phonic skills.

Improving Comprehension 6-7 © A & C Black Publications Ltd. 2008

Sheba and the dragon

Name: _____

Date: _____

Answer the questions by completing the sentences.

What did Sheba and her friends like to do all day long?

Sheba and her friends liked to _____

_____ all day long.

After her friends had gone, who did Sheba see in the field?

Sheba saw a _____

How did the dragon feel?

The dragon felt very _____

Write sentences to answer the next questions.

How did Sheba find her friends?

_____

_____

Why do you think the dragon licked his lips?

_____

_____

Did the dragon like the grass when he tried it?

_____

_____

Notes for teachers

The partly written answers give clues to the missing words. The purpose of this is to familiarise children with different styles of questions. Encourage the children to plan what they are going to write before they do so. Discourage them from answering the final question with just one word but instead to write a complete sentence.

Improving Comprehension 6-7 © A & C Black Publications Ltd. 2008

Sheba and the dragon

Name: _____

Date: _____

Answer the questions by completing the sentences.

Which two words describe how Sheba was eating?

Sheba was _____

Why did Sheba not notice that her friends had gone?

Sheba did not notice that her friends were gone because

_____

Write sentences to answer these questions.

How did Sheba stop the dragon from eating her?

_____

_____

How did Sheba find her friends again?

_____

_____

How did the sheep stop the dragon from eating them?

_____

_____

If you saw a dragon what would you do?

_____

_____

Notes for teachers
Read the passage with the children and discuss what happened in the story and how the sheep ended up tricking the dragon. The last question provides an opportunity for the children to be creative and the answer could be extended to create their own story about a dragon.

Jig Snaps

The tasty breakfast cereal made from wheat and other natural ingredients.

Eat Jig Snaps for breakfast fun.
Two Jig Snaps = one great shape.
Find all ten Jig Snap shapes in your bowl.

Eat them on their own or with milk.
Three great flavours – honey – banana – chocolate.

Buy a box of Jig Snaps today.
Buy two boxes and get this free Jig Snaps bowl.

Improving Comprehension 6-7 © A & C Black Publications Ltd. 2008

Jig Snaps

Name: _____

Date: _____

Put a ring round each of the correct answers.

What are Jig Snaps?

sweets   puzzles   breakfast cereal   tea-time treat

What might you put on your Jig Snaps?

tea   milk   orange juice   bananas

Jig Snaps are made from

wheat   barley   chocolate   oats

Answer the next question by filling in the spaces

What are the three Jig Snaps flavours?

The three flavours are _____ ,

_____ and _____.

What do you eat for breakfast? Draw a picture of you eating breakfast. Write about your picture.

_____

_____

_____

_____

_____

Notes for teachers
Read the page about Jig Snaps with the children helping them to understand that it is an advertisement and how you know this from the layout of the page and the use of language. The final question is to promote discussion. Encourage children to write one or two clear sentences using capital letters and full stops in the correct places.

Improving Comprehension 6-7 © A & C Black Publications Ltd. 2008

Jig Snaps

Name: _____

Date: _____

Answer the questions by completing the sentences.

How many Jig Snaps pieces make each shape?

Each shape is made from _____

For what meal would you eat Jig Snaps?

You would eat _____

When does the advert say you should buy a box
of Jig Snaps?

The advert says _____

Answer the next questions by writing whole sentences.

How many Jig Snaps characters are there?

_____

_____

What is the main ingredient used to make Jig Snaps?

_____

_____

In what two ways would you eat Jig Snaps?

_____

_____

_____

Notes for teachers
Read the page about Jig Snaps with the children helping them to understand that it is an advertisement and
how you know this from the use of language and how the page is laid out. Help them to write their answers
neatly, using complete sentences and appropriate punctuation.

Jig Snaps

Name: _____

Date: _____

Make a list of the ten items you can make with Jig Snaps.

_____   _____

_____   _____

_____   _____

_____   _____

_____   _____

What special offer is on the advert?

_____

_____

What are Jig Snaps made from?

_____

_____

Jig Snaps come in three flavours; banana, chocolate and honey. Name one more flavour you think would be tasty.

_____

Draw three more characters that could be made from Jig Snaps pieces.

Notes for teachers
Read the page about Jig Snaps through with the children helping them to understand that it is an advertisement. In answering the second question 'wheat' and 'other natural ingredients' should be included. When thinking about another flavour, ask pupils to consider what flavours would be enjoyed every day by a lot of people and could be eaten with milk. In the final task pupils should be encouraged to consider thinking about shapes that have no thin / long pieces that could break easily in the box.

Improving Comprehension 6-7 © A & C Black Publications Ltd. 2008

A fable

A fable is a story with a lesson. The lesson to be learned from this story is to 'look before you leap'.

A fox was running across the grass. As he ran he tripped and fell into a deep dark well. He tried to climb out but the well was deep and the sides were steep. He was stuck.

A little later an old goat came along looking for some water to drink. The fox made a plan to get out of the well. He would play a trick on the goat.

The goat looked down into the well. It was dark and he could not see much down there.

"Hello," said the goat. "I am very thirsty, is there any water down there in the well?"

"Oh yes," replied the fox. "There is lovely cool clear water down here. Why don't you come and have some?"

The goat jumped down into the well and had a drink. Then he looked up and saw that he couldn't climb out again.

The fox jumped up onto the goat's back and from there climbed out of the well.

"How can I get out again?" asked the goat.

"You should have thought about that before you jumped in," laughed the fox as he ran off.

Improving Comprehension 6-7 © A & C Black Publications Ltd. 2008

A fable

Look before you leap

Name: _____

Date: _____

Put a ring round each of the correct answers.

Which animal fell down the well?

goat   rabbit   fox   dog

What was the goat looking for?

food   the fox   water   the well

Who laughed at the end of the story?

The fox   The goat   The rabbit   The dog

Complete the sentences by filling in the spaces.

The fox was running across the _____ when he fell into the well.

The fox jumped onto the goat's _____ to climb out of the well.

Draw a picture of the goat having a drink when he was first in the well. Write about your picture.

_____

_____

_____

Notes for teachers
In the first question you may need to remind the children that the goat climbed down into the well, he didn't fall into it. Discuss the final question and then encourage children to write one or two clear sentences using capital letters and full stops in the correct places.

A fable

Name: _____

Date: _____

Answer the questions by completing the sentences.

How did the fox get out of the well?

To get out of the well, the fox _____

_____

What lesson can be learned from the story?

The lesson from the story is look _____

How did the fox become stuck in the well?

The fox fell into the well when he _____

_____

Write whole sentences to answer the next questions.

Who played a trick on the goat?

_____

Who was in the well at the end of the story?

_____

How many characters are in the story?

_____

_____

Which do you think was the cleverer character in this story?

_____

_____

_____

Notes for teachers

Read the passage through with the children. Help them to understand what has happened in the story and discuss some examples of how the message in the story could be applied to every day life.

Improving Comprehension 6-7 © A & C Black Publications Ltd. 2008

A fable
'Look before you leap.'

Name: _____

Date: _____

Write a sentence to explain why the lesson of this story is 'look before you leap'.

_____

_____

Write two words used to describe the well.

_____   _____

Write two words used to describe the water.

_____   _____

Put the two halves of each sentence together correctly.

The first one has been done for you.

The poor old goat was	he heard a goat coming along.
The fox thought he was stuck until	left in the well.
One day a fox was running across a field when	there was water to drink in the well.
He told the thirsty goat	onto the goat's back.
He climbed out by jumping	fell into a deep dark well.

On a separate piece of paper write the sentences in the correct order. Draw a picture to go with the story.

Notes for teachers
Read the passage through with the children and see if they can explain what has happened in the story. An extension activity would be to talk to pupils about how the story illustrates the saying 'look before you leap' and to ask them to make up other stories with the same lesson.

Improving Comprehension 6-7 © A & C Black Publications Ltd. 2008

The beach

Run to the beach,
Sun all the day.

Tide going out,
Slide on the rocks.

Paddling in the surf,
Dabbling in rock pools.

Splashing in the water,
Crashing of the waves.

Wide stretch of sand,
Ride on a donkey.

Crying of the gulls,
Flying in the air.

Buying an ice cream.
Trying to build castles.

Hand feeling for shells,
Sand trickling through fingers.

Sun going down,
Fun at an end.

Improving Comprehension 6-7 © A & C Black Publications Ltd. 2008

The beach

Name: _____

Date: _____

Put a ring round each of the correct answers.

What is the poem called?

The beach   The sea   The waves   The rocks

What flies in the air?

children   gulls   rocks   sun

What food is in the poem?

cake   cream   orange   ice cream

Answer the next questions by filling in the spaces

On the beach sometimes people can ride on a

_____.

Children may build _____ made from sand.

Draw a picture of you playing at the seaside. Write a sentence about your picture.

_____

_____

_____

_____

Notes for teachers
Read the poem through with the children. Do they notice that it doesn't rhyme? Help them to understand that it is still a poem and it can be read to a beat. The most important aspect of the poem, though, is that it should encourage the reader/listener to picture the scene described. The pupils may notice that there are rhyming words but these occur at the start of each pair of lines rather than at the end. They might need some explanation of the last line.

Improving Comprehension 6-7 © A & C Black Publications Ltd. 2008

The beach

Name: _____

Date: _____

Answer the questions by completing the sentences.

How many verses are there in the poem?

There are _____

What animal could you ride on, on the beach?

You could ride on a _____

Answer the next questions by writing whole sentences.

Where are the gulls in the poem?

_____

_____

When is it time to finish playing on the beach?

_____

_____

What might you buy to eat on the beach?

_____

_____

Look in the poem to find the words that rhyme with each of the words below.

run _____   wide _____

sand _____   buying _____

Notes for teachers
Read the poem through with the children. Do they notice that it doesn't rhyme? Help the children to understand that it is still a poem and it can be read to a beat. The most important aspect of the poem, though, is that it should encourage the reader/listener to picture the scene described. Help the pupils to notice that there are some rhyming words but they occur at the start of each pair of lines rather than at the end.

Name: _____

Date: _____

What three things tell you that this is a poem?

1 _____

2 _____

3 _____

What is unusual about the way the poem rhymes?

_____

_____

Find a word from the box to rhyme with each pair of rhyming words from the poem. If you can, write an extra rhyming word for each set.

splashing	crashing	_____	_____
buying	crying	_____	_____
tide	slide	_____	_____
hand	sand	_____	_____
sun	fun	_____	_____

planned   cried   dashing   sighing   stun

Notes for teachers
Things that could be mentioned in the answer to the first question include: short lines (not sentences), capital letters at the beginning of each line, text set out in pairs of lines/verses, or the rhyming evident. The answer to the third question should indicate the rhyming words being at the beginning of each line rather than the end.

Improving Comprehension 6-7 © A & C Black Publications Ltd. 2008

Holiday snaps

Connor had been on holiday with his mum and dad and his big sister Gemma. It was the first time he had been on a plane to another country. Granny and Grandad had given him a camera to take some pictures. Here is a page from his photo album.

I liked flying on the plane to Spain. When I looked out of the window we were over the Isle of Wight. We were on the plane for about two and a half hours. I was very excited when we landed in Spain.

We stayed in a lovely house that is called a villa. There was one bedroom for Mum and Dad, one bedroom for Gemma and one for me! In the garden was a swimming pool just for us. I went for a swim every day.

There was a stone table near the pool so we had our meals outside nearly every day. There were high palm trees near the table.

There was a lovely beach and a very big rock near our villa. I thought the rock looked like a shark with a great big mouth. We had fun playing on the beach.

Improving Comprehension 6-7 © A & C Black Publications Ltd. 2008

Holiday snaps

Name: _____

Date: _____

Put a ring round each of the correct answers.

Where did Connor go on holiday?

Beach   Spain   France   England

The house was called a

home   valley   house   villa

What was the name of Connor's sister?

Gill   Gail   Gemma   Jemima

Complete the sentences by filling in the spaces.

The big rock looked like a _____ with a very big mouth.

There was a _____ _____ in the garden.

Have you ever been on a holiday? Draw a picture of a holiday or a day out that you have had. Write about your picture.

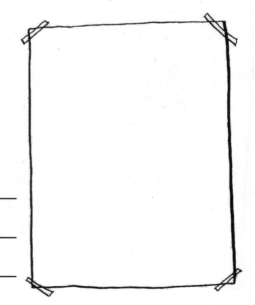

_____

_____

_____

Notes for teachers
Read the text with the children helping them to understand that it is a page from Connor's photo album and that he has written the text to go with each photo. Discuss the last question with the children and help them compose some sentences orally before writing anything down.

Improving Comprehension 6-7 © A & C Black Publications Ltd. 2008

Holiday snaps

Name: _____

Date: _____

Answer the questions by completing the sentences.

How many bedrooms were in the villa?

There were _____

_____

What does the first photograph show?

The first photograph shows _____

_____

How long did the journey to Spain take?

The journey to Spain took about _____

_____

Answer the next questions by writing whole sentences.

What did the rock look like?

_____

_____

What was near the stone table?

_____

_____

Who gave Connor the camera to take his pictures with?

_____

_____

Notes for teachers
Read the text with the children helping them to understand that it is a page from Connor's photo album and that he has written the text to go with each photo. Discuss the questions and encourage the children to punctuate their answers correctly, using capital letters and full stops in the appropriate places.

Improving Comprehension 6-7 © A & C Black Publications Ltd. 2008

Holiday snaps

Name: _____

Date: _____

The title of the text is 'Holiday Snaps'. Explain what is meant by the word 'snaps'.

_____

_____

How many people went on holiday and who were they?

_____

_____

What was the name of the island that Connor saw when he looked out of the window of the plane?

_____

_____

What do you think the weather was like on Connor's holiday? Explain how you know.

_____

_____

_____

On a separate piece of paper write about where you would like to go on holiday.

Notes for teachers
Where appropriate, questions should be answered in complete sentences. Ensure that pupils understand that the word 'snaps' is another word for photographs. When answering the question about the weather on the holiday ensure pupils refer to the text in their answer, i.e. 'I think that the weather was hot because Connor went swimming every day' is acceptable. 'I think that the weather was hot because I have been to Spain' is not acceptable.

Improving Comprehension 6-7 © A & C Black Publications Ltd. 2008